# TIMES TABLES

×3

10 x 5 = 50

| 6 | × | 3 | = | 18 |
| 5 | × | 5 | = | 25 |
| 8 | × | 7 | = | 56 |
| 4 | × | 2 | =.....? |
| 1 | × | 10 | =.....? |
| 2 | × | 9 | =.....? |

1 x 3 = 3

5 x 2 = 10

7 x 8 = 56

2 x 2 = 4

6 x 5 = 30

5 x 1 = 5

1 x 2 = 2

## PLUS Pull-out Poster!

**Brown Watson**

ENGLAND

# Times Tables - x1, x2, x3, x4, x5

**x1**

| | | | | |
|---|---|---|---|---|
| 1 | x | 1 | = | 1 |
| 2 | x | 1 | = | 2 |
| 3 | x | 1 | = | 3 |
| 4 | x | 1 | = | 4 |
| 5 | x | 1 | = | 5 |
| 6 | x | 1 | = | 6 |
| 7 | x | 1 | = | 7 |
| 8 | x | 1 | = | 8 |
| 9 | x | 1 | = | 9 |
| 10 | x | 1 | = | 10 |

**x2**

| | | | | |
|---|---|---|---|---|
| 1 | x | 2 | = | 2 |
| 2 | x | 2 | = | 4 |
| 3 | x | 2 | = | 6 |
| 4 | x | 2 | = | 8 |
| 5 | x | 2 | = | 10 |
| 6 | x | 2 | = | 12 |
| 7 | x | 2 | = | 14 |
| 8 | x | 2 | = | 16 |
| 9 | x | 2 | = | 18 |
| 10 | x | 2 | = | 20 |

**x3**

| | | | | |
|---|---|---|---|---|
| 1 | x | 3 | = | 3 |
| 2 | x | 3 | = | 6 |
| 3 | x | 3 | = | 9 |
| 4 | x | 3 | = | 12 |
| 5 | x | 3 | = | 15 |
| 6 | x | 3 | = | 18 |
| 7 | x | 3 | = | 21 |
| 8 | x | 3 | = | 24 |
| 9 | x | 3 | = | 27 |
| 10 | x | 3 | = | 30 |

**x4**

| | | | | |
|---|---|---|---|---|
| 1 | x | 4 | = | 4 |
| 2 | x | 4 | = | 8 |
| 3 | x | 4 | = | 12 |
| 4 | x | 4 | = | 16 |
| 5 | x | 4 | = | 20 |
| 6 | x | 4 | = | 24 |
| 7 | x | 4 | = | 28 |
| 8 | x | 4 | = | 32 |
| 9 | x | 4 | = | 36 |
| 10 | x | 4 | = | 40 |

**x5**

| | | | | |
|---|---|---|---|---|
| 1 | x | 5 | = | 5 |
| 2 | x | 5 | = | 10 |
| 3 | x | 5 | = | 15 |
| 4 | x | 5 | = | 20 |
| 5 | x | 5 | = | 25 |
| 6 | x | 5 | = | 30 |
| 7 | x | 5 | = | 35 |
| 8 | x | 5 | = | 40 |
| 9 | x | 5 | = | 45 |
| 10 | x | 5 | = | 50 |

# Times Tables - x6, x7, x8, x9, x10

**x6**

| | | | | |
|---|---|---|---|---|
| 1 | x | 6 | = | 6 |
| 2 | x | 6 | = | 12 |
| 3 | x | 6 | = | 18 |
| 4 | x | 6 | = | 24 |
| 5 | x | 6 | = | 30 |
| 6 | x | 6 | = | 36 |
| 7 | x | 6 | = | 42 |
| 8 | x | 6 | = | 48 |
| 9 | x | 6 | = | 54 |
| 10 | x | 6 | = | 60 |

**x7**

| | | | | |
|---|---|---|---|---|
| 1 | x | 7 | = | 7 |
| 2 | x | 7 | = | 14 |
| 3 | x | 7 | = | 21 |
| 4 | x | 7 | = | 28 |
| 5 | x | 7 | = | 35 |
| 6 | x | 7 | = | 42 |
| 7 | x | 7 | = | 49 |
| 8 | x | 7 | = | 56 |
| 9 | x | 7 | = | 63 |
| 10 | x | 7 | = | 70 |

**x8**

| | | | | |
|---|---|---|---|---|
| 1 | x | 8 | = | 8 |
| 2 | x | 8 | = | 16 |
| 3 | x | 8 | = | 24 |
| 4 | x | 8 | = | 32 |
| 5 | x | 8 | = | 40 |
| 6 | x | 8 | = | 48 |
| 7 | x | 8 | = | 56 |
| 8 | x | 8 | = | 64 |
| 9 | x | 8 | = | 72 |
| 10 | x | 8 | = | 80 |

**x9**

| | | | | |
|---|---|---|---|---|
| 1 | x | 9 | = | 9 |
| 2 | x | 9 | = | 18 |
| 3 | x | 9 | = | 27 |
| 4 | x | 9 | = | 36 |
| 5 | x | 9 | = | 45 |
| 6 | x | 9 | = | 54 |
| 7 | x | 9 | = | 63 |
| 8 | x | 9 | = | 72 |
| 9 | x | 9 | = | 81 |
| 10 | x | 9 | = | 90 |

**x10**

| | | | | |
|---|---|---|---|---|
| 1 | x | 10 | = | 10 |
| 2 | x | 10 | = | 20 |
| 3 | x | 10 | = | 30 |
| 4 | x | 10 | = | 40 |
| 5 | x | 10 | = | 50 |
| 6 | x | 10 | = | 60 |
| 7 | x | 10 | = | 70 |
| 8 | x | 10 | = | 80 |
| 9 | x | 10 | = | 90 |
| 10 | x | 10 | = | 100 |

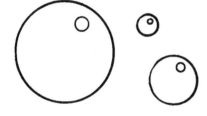
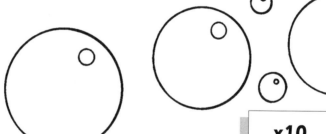

# 1 times table

Multiply any number by 1 (x1) and that number will always stay the same.

Divide any number by 1 (÷1) and that number stays the same.

Write the correct answers in the spaces provided.

| | | | | | |
|---|---|---|---|---|---|
| **1** | x | 1 | = | **1** | |
| **2** | x | 1 | = | **2** | |
| **3** | x | 1 | = | 3 | |
| **4** | x | 1 | = | 4 | |
| **5** | x | 1 | = | 5 | |
| **6** | x | 1 | = | 6 | |
| **7** | x | 1 | = | 7 | |
| **8** | x | 1 | = | 8 | |
| **9** | x | 1 | = | 9 | |
| **10** | x | 1 | = | 10 | |

| | | | | | |
|---|---|---|---|---|---|
| 1 | x | **1** | = | **1** | |
| 1 | x | **2** | = | **2** | |
| 1 | x | **3** | = | 3 | |
| 1 | x | **4** | = | 4 | |
| 1 | x | **5** | = | 5 | |
| 1 | x | **6** | = | 6 | |
| 1 | x | **7** | = | 7 | |
| 1 | x | **8** | = | 8 | |
| 1 | x | **9** | = | 9 | |
| 1 | x | **10** | = | 10 | |

| | | | | | |
|---|---|---|---|---|---|
| 2 | x | 1 | = | 2 | |
| 1 | x | 8 | = | 8 | |
| 5 | ÷ | 1 | = | 5 | |
| 1 | ÷ | 1 | = | 1 | |
| 4 | x | 1 | = | 4 | |
| 7 | x | 1 | = | 7 | |
| 1 | x | 3 | = | 3 | |
| 10 | ÷ | 1 | = | 10 | |
| 6 | ÷ | 1 | = | 6 | |
| 1 | x | 9 | = | 9 | |

☺ Any number multiplied by 1 (x 1) stays the same

# Flying kites!

Which kite belongs to which kite-flyer?
First do the sums. Then draw a string connecting each child with his or her kite.

## 2 times table

2 is an even number.
All even numbers end in 2, 4, 6, 8 or 0. Any even number can be divided by 2.

Write the correct answers in the spaces provided.

| | | |
|---|---|---|
| 1 x 2 = 1 | 1 x 2 = **2** | 2 ÷ 2 = **1** |
| 2 x 2 = 2 | 2 x 2 = **4** | 4 ÷ 2 = ..... |
| 3 x 2 = 3 | 3 x 2 = **6** | 6 ÷ .... = ..... |
| 4 x 2 = 4 | 4 x 2 = **8** | ..... ÷ 2 = ..... |
| 5 x 2 = 5 | 5 x 2 = **10** | 10 ÷ 2 = ..... |
| 6 x 2 = 6 | 6 x 2 = **12** | 12 ÷ .... = ..... |
| 7 x 2 = 7 | 7 x 2 = **14** | ..... ÷ .... = **7** |
| 8 x 2 = 8 | 8 x 2 = **16** | ..... ÷ 2 = **8** |
| 9 x 2 = 9 | 9 x 2 = **18** | 18 ÷ .... = ..... |
| 10 x 2 = 10 | 10 x 2 = **20** | 20 ÷ .... = ..... |

☺ Any times table (multiplication = X) is a quick way of adding up.

# Two in a pair

Here is a group of puppets. Draw a circle around each pair.
(The first has been done for you.)   How many pairs are there?

How many pairs?   2

How many in each pair?   10

How many puppets?   20

How many puppets in 4 pairs?   **(4 pairs  x  2 puppets = 8 )**

How many puppets in 8 pairs?   16

How many puppets in 6 pairs?   12

😊  All numbers in the 2 times (2x) table end in 2, 4, 6, 8 or 0

# x 3

## 3 times table

3 is an odd number.

Your 3 times (3x) table makes dividing by 3 (÷3) easy!

Write the correct answers in the spaces provided.

| | | | | | |
|---|---|---|---|---|---|
| **1** | x | 3 | = | **3** |
| **2** | x | 3 | = | **6** |
| **3** | x | 3 | = | 9 |
| **4** | x | 3 | = | 12 |
| **5** | x | 3 | = | 15 |
| **6** | x | 3 | = | 18 |
| **7** | x | 3 | = | 21 |
| **8** | x | 3 | = | 24 |
| **9** | x | 3 | = | 27 |
| **10** | x | 3 | = | 30 |

| | | | | | |
|---|---|---|---|---|---|
| **1** | x | 3 | = | **3** |
| **2** | x | 3 | = | **6** |
| **3** | x | 3 | = | **9** |
| ..... | x | 3 | = | **12** |
| **5** | x | ..... | = | **15** |
| ..... | x | 3 | = | **18** |
| **7** | x | ..... | = | **21** |
| ..... | x | 3 | = | **24** |
| ..... | x | 3 | = | **27** |
| **10** | x | ..... | = | **30** |

| | | | | | |
|---|---|---|---|---|---|
| **3** | ÷ | 3 | = | 1 |
| **6** | ÷ | 3 | = | ..... |
| **9** | ÷ | ..... | = | **3** |
| **12** | ÷ | 3 | = | ..... |
| **15** | ÷ | 3 | = | ..... |
| **18** | ÷ | ..... | = | ..... |
| ..... | ÷ | ..... | = | **7** |
| ..... | ÷ | 3 | = | ..... |
| **27** | ÷ | ..... | = | ...... |
| **30** | ÷ | ..... | = | **10** |

☺ Three is an odd number

# Think in threes!

3 Bears

3 Billy Goats Gruff

3 Little Pigs

3 Little Kittens

3 Blind Mice

3 Little Fishes

3 Wise Monkeys

How many groups of 3 animals are there?   There are ..7.. groups of 3s

How many animals in 3 groups of 3?          3 x 3    = ..... animals

How many animals in 4 groups of 3?          4 x 3    = ..... animals

How many animals in 5 groups of 3?          5 x 3    = ..... animals

How many animals in 7 groups of 3?          7 x 3    = ..... animals

How many animals in 9 groups of 3?          9 x 3    = ..... animals

How many animals are there on this page?    ...x 3   = ..... animals

☺  Any times table (multiplication = x) is a quick way of adding up.

## 4 times table

4 is an even number.
Any even number can be divided by 2.

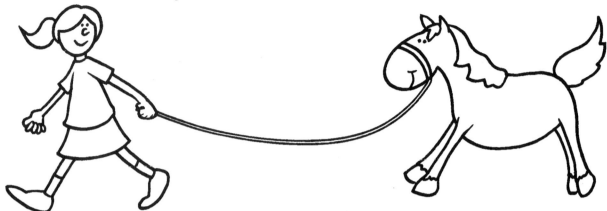

Write the correct answers in the spaces provided.

| | | |
|---|---|---|
| 1 x 4 = **4** | 1 x 4 = **4** | 4 ÷ 4 = **1** |
| 2 x 4 = **8** | 2 x 4 = **8** | 8 ÷ 4 = **2** |
| 3 x 4 = 12 | 3 x ….= **12** | ….÷ 4 = ….. |
| 4 x 4 = 16 | ….x 4 = **16** | ….÷ 4 = ….. |
| 5 x 4 = 20 | 5 x ….= **20** | 20 ÷ ….= **5** |
| 6 x 4 = 24 | ….x 4 = **24** | 24 ÷ ….= ….. |
| 7 x 4 = 28 | 7 x ….= **28** | ….÷ ….= ….. |
| 8 x 4 = 32 | ….x 4 = **32** | ….÷ 4 = **8** |
| 9 x 4 = 36 | ….x 4 = **36** | 36 ÷ ….= ….. |
| 10 x 4 = 40 | 10 x ….= **40** | 40 ÷ ….= ….. |

☺ All even numbers end in 2, 4, 6, 8 or 0

# How many horseshoes?

dad!

A horse has **4** legs

So it needs **4** horseshoes

Count up the number of horses in the field. How many are there? Write the answer.

There are ..... horses in the field.

Each horse needs ..... horseshoes.

### Can you finish this table?

1 horse needs ..8.. horseshoes
..... horses need ..7.. horseshoes
..... horses need ..6.. horseshoes
..... horses need ..5.. horseshoes
..... horses need ..4.. horseshoes
..... horses need ..3.. horseshoes
..... horses need ..2.. horseshoes
..... horses need ..1.. horseshoes

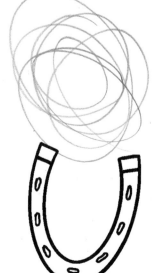

**Now count the horseshoes on this page.**
There are ..6.. horseshoes.
These are enough for ..0.. horses.

 Multiplication is a quick way of adding up!

# x 5

## 5 times table

5 is a special number.
Any number multiplied by 5 (x5) ends in **0** or **5**.

Write the correct answers in the spaces provided.

| | | | |
|---|---|---|---|
| **1** x **5** = | **5** |
| **2** x **5** = | **10** |
| **3** x **5** = | 15 |
| **4** x **5** = | 20 |
| **5** x **5** = | 25 |
| **6** x **5** = | 30 |
| **7** x **5** = | 35 |
| **8** x **5** = | 40 |
| **9** x **5** = | 45 |
| **10** x **5** = | 50 |

| | | | |
|---|---|---|---|
| **1** x **5** = | **5** |
| **2** x **5** = | **10** |
| **3** x 5 = | **15** |
| 4 x **5** = | **20** |
| **5** x 5 = | **25** |
| 6 x **5** = | **30** |
| **7** x 5 = | **35** |
| 8 x **5** = | **40** |
| 9 x **5** = | **45** |
| **10** x 5 = | **50** |

| | | | |
|---|---|---|---|
| **5** ÷ **5** = | **1** |
| **10** ÷ **5** = | **2** |
| **15** ÷ 5 = | 3 |
| 20 ÷ **5** = | 4 |
| **25** ÷ **5** = | 5 |
| **30** ÷ 5 = | 6 |
| 35 ÷ 5 = | **7** |
| 40 ÷ **5** = | **8** |
| **45** ÷ 5 = | 9 |
| **50** ÷ 5 = | 10 |

☺ ANY number times 5 (x5) ends in 0 or 5

# Meet the quins!

Quins are 5 babies all born at the same time, to the same mother.
And quins need 5 times as many things as 1 baby to keep them happy!
Can you divide all the things between them, so that each one gets the same?

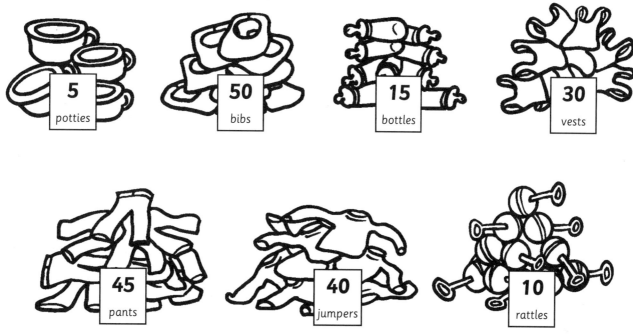

| | | | |
|---|---|---|---|
| 5 potties | 50 bibs | 15 bottles | 30 vests |
| 45 pants | 40 jumpers | 10 rattles | |

Each baby needs -

5.... potty      5o bibs      15. bottles

3o. vests      45 pants      4o. jumpers      1o. rattles

☺  Five is a special number

☺  Any number divided by 5 (÷5) must end in 0 or 5

## 6 times table

6 is an even number.

Write the correct answers in the spaces provided.

| | | |
|---|---|---|
| **1** x 6 = **6** | **1** x 6 = **6** | **6** ÷ 6 = **1** |
| **2** x 6 = **12** | **2** x 6 = **12** | **12** ÷ 6 = ..... |
| **3** x 6 = ..... | **3** x 6 = **18** | .....÷ 6 = ..... |
| **4** x 6 = ..... | .....x 6 = **24** | .....÷ 6 = ..... |
| **5** x 6 = ..... | **5** x .....= **30** | **30** ÷ .....= **5** |
| **6** x 6 = ..... | .....x 6 = **36** | **36** ÷ .....= ..... |
| **7** x 6 = ..... | **7** x ....= **42** | .....÷ .....= ..... |
| **8** x 6 = ..... | .....x 6 = **48** | .....÷ 6 = **8** |
| **9** x 6 = ..... | .....x 6 = **54** | **54** ÷ .....= ..... |
| **10** x 6 = ..... | **10** x ....= **60** | **60** ÷ .....= ..... |

☺ All even numbers can be divided by 2

# 1 beetle, 6 legs

A black beetle is an insect; and, like all insects, it has **6** legs.
Here is a line of 3 black beetles, each one needing six legs.

How many legs did you draw in total?

Write out the sum          .......... beetles x 6 legs = ........

Here are some more black beetles for you to finish.

.......... beetles x 6 legs = ........

.......... beetles x 6 legs = ........

.......... beetles x 6 legs = ........

☺ Remember! Multiplication (x) is a quick way of adding up!

## 7 times table

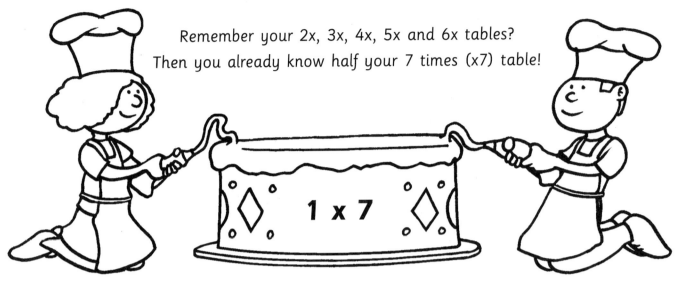

Remember your 2x, 3x, 4x, 5x and 6x tables?
Then you already know half your 7 times (x7) table!

1 x 7

Write the correct answers in the spaces provided.

| | | |
|---|---|---|
| 1 x 7 = **7** | 1 x 7 = **7** | 7 ÷ 7 = **1** |
| 2 x 7 = **14** | 2 x 7 = **14** | 14 ÷ 7 = ..... |
| 3 x 7 = ..... | 3 x .....= **21** | .....÷ 7 = ..... |
| 4 x 7 = ..... | .....x 7 = **28** | .....÷ 7 = ..... |
| 5 x 7 = ..... | 5 x .....= **35** | 35 ÷ .....= ..... |
| 6 x 7 = ..... | .....x 7 = **42** | 42 ÷ .....= ..... |
| 7 x 7 = ..... | 7 x .....= **49** | .....÷ .....= ..... |
| 8 x 7 = ..... | .....x 7 = **56** | .....÷ 7 = ..... |
| 9 x 7 = ..... | .....x 7 = **63** | 63 ÷ .....= ..... |
| 10 x 7 = ..... | 10 x .....= **70** | 70 ÷ .....= ..... |

☺ Any times table (multiplication = x) is a quick way of adding up.

# Cake Mix

Jake's friends are each making cakes for his birthday party.
Can you work out who is making which cake?

Emma is making ................  Dan is making ................

Jill is making ................  Mark is making ................

Beth is making ................  Joe is making ................

☺ Remember! Multiplication tables (x) make division (÷) easy!

## 8 times table

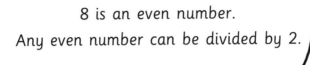

8 is an even number.
Any even number can be divided by 2.

Write the correct answers in the spaces provided.

| | | |
|---|---|---|
| **1** x **8** = **8** | **1** x **8** = **8** | **8** ÷ **8** = **1** |
| **2** x **8** = **16** | **2** x **8** = **16** | **16** ÷ ..... = ..... |
| **3** x **8** = ..... | **3** x ..... = **24** | ..... ÷ **8** = ..... |
| **4** x **8** = ..... | ..... x **8** = **32** | ..... ÷ **8** = ..... |
| **5** x **8** = ..... | **5** x ..... = **40** | **40** ÷ ..... = **5** |
| **6** x **8** = ..... | ..... x **8** = **48** | **48** ÷ ..... = ..... |
| **7** x **8** = ..... | **7** x ..... = **56** | ..... ÷ ..... = ..... |
| **8** x **8** = ..... | ..... x **8** = **64** | **64** ÷ ..... = **8** |
| **9** x **8** = ..... | ..... x **8** = **72** | **72** ÷ ..... = ..... |
| **10** x **8** = ..... | **10** x ..... = **80** | **80** ÷ ..... = ..... |

☺ All even numbers end in 2, 4, 6, 8 or 0

# Octopus legs

You know that an octopus has 8 legs.

How many legs are there on 3 octopus?

Write the sum first.

3 octopus x 8 legs = 24

How many legs on 5 octopus?     How many legs on 7 octopus?

..... octopus  x  ..... legs  =  .....     ..... octopus  x  ..... legs  =  .....

A spider has 8 legs, too. Draw 8 legs for each spider.

How many spiders are there?     There are ..... spiders.

How many legs did you draw in total?     .....

Write the sum.     ..... spiders  x  ..... legs  =  .....

☺ Any times table (multiplication = x) is a quick way of adding up

## 9 times table

9 is an odd number.

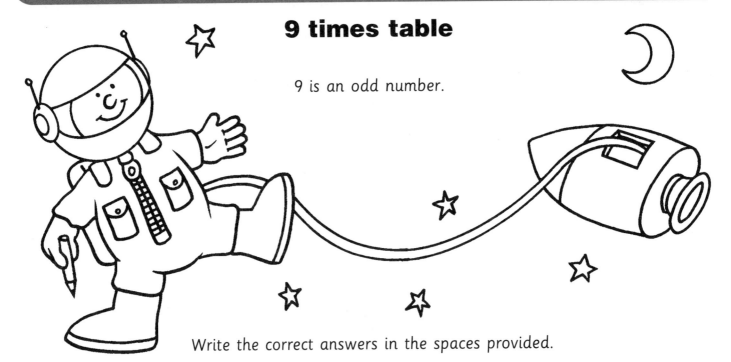

Write the correct answers in the spaces provided.

| | | | |
|---|---|---|---|
| 1 x 9 = **9** | 1 x 9 = **9** | 9 ÷ 9 = **1** |
| 2 x 9 = **18** | 2 x 9 = **18** | 18 ÷ 9 = ..... |
| 3 x 9 = ..... | 3 x .....= **27** | .....÷ 9 = ..... |
| 4 x 9 = ..... | .....x 9 = **36** | .....÷ 9 = ..... |
| 5 x 9 = ..... | 5 x .....= ..... | 45 ÷ .....= **5** |
| 6 x 9 = ..... | .....x 9 = **54** | .....÷ 9 = ..... |
| 7 x 9 = ..... | .....x .....= ..... | .....÷ .....= **7** |
| 8 x 9 = ..... | .....x 9 = ..... | 72 ÷ .....= ..... |
| 9 x 9 = ..... | .....x 9 = ..... | .....÷ .....= **9** |
| 10 x 9 = ..... | 10 x .....= **90** | 90 ÷ .....= ..... |

☺ The nine times table (x9) rocket countdown will help you!

# Countdown to 9 times table (x9)

The 9x table rocket is here to help you!

Count **up** on the left

Count **down** on the right

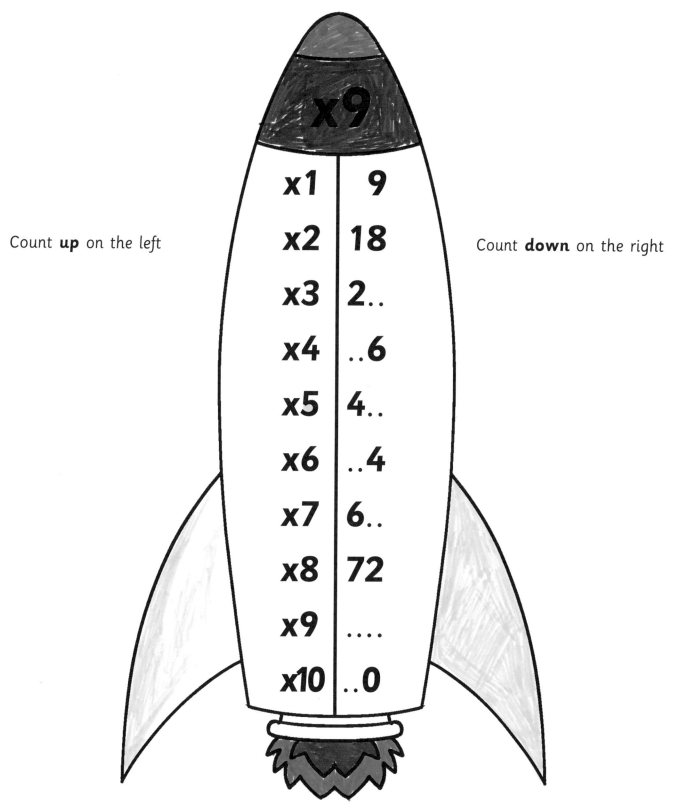

| x9 | |
|---|---|
| x1 | 9 |
| x2 | 18 |
| x3 | 2.. |
| x4 | ..6 |
| x5 | 4.. |
| x6 | ..4 |
| x7 | 6.. |
| x8 | 72 |
| x9 | .... |
| x10 | ..0 |

Fill in the rest of the numbers and you have
written down your 9 times (9x) table.

# x 10

## 10 times table

10 is a special number!
Any number multiplied by 10 (x 10) ends in 0.

18 x 10 = 180

Write the correct answers in the spaces provided.

| | | |
|---|---|---|
| 1 x 10 = **10** | 1 x 10 = **10** | 10 ÷ 10 = **1** |
| 2 x 10 = **20** | 2 x 10 = **20** | 20 ÷ 10 = 2 |
| 3 x 10 = 30 | 3 x 10 = **30** | 30 ÷ 10 = 3 |
| 4 x 10 = 40 | 4 x 10 = 40 | 40 ÷ 10 = 4 |
| 5 x 10 = 50 | 5 x 10 = **50** | 50 ÷ 10 = 5 |
| 6 x 10 = 60 | 6 x 10 = 60 | 60 ÷ 10 = 6 |
| 7 x 10 = 70 | 7 x 10 = 70 | 70 ÷ 10 = 7 |
| 8 x 10 = 80 | 8 x 10 = 80 | 80 ÷ 10 = 8 |
| 9 x 10 = 90 | 9 x 10 = 90 | 90 ÷ 10 = 9 |
| 10 x 10 = 100 | 10 x 10 = 100 | 100 ÷ 10 = 10 |

☺ All numbers ending in 0 can be divided by 10

# Clever Ten!

Class 10 is clever - because the 'clever tens' never forget the **easy way to multiply by 10** (x10) is to add **0**.

6x10 = 60

8x10 = 80

3x10 = 30

1x10 = 10 ✓

4x10 = 40

☺ Any number multiplied by 10 (x10) ends in 0

# Up in a balloon

But, where will it land? In this puzzle, each sum equals a letter. As you do each sum, cross the letter off the list and the number off the balloon.
Put the letters which remain into the right order to spell out the place where the balloon comes down to earth.

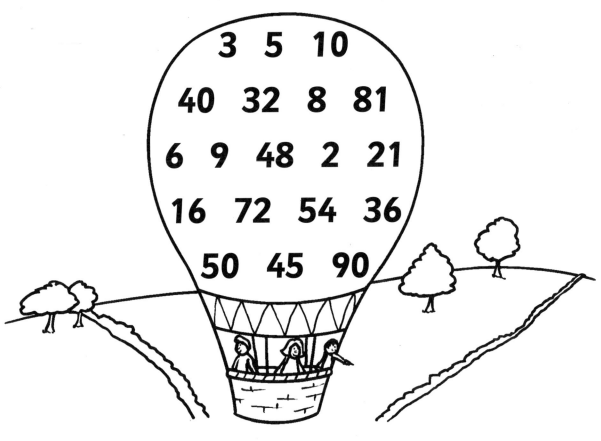

| | | | | | | | | | | | |
|---|---|---|---|---|---|---|---|---|---|---|---|
| **A** | 6 | x | 4 | = | ..... | **N** | 7 | x | 6 | = | ..... |
| **B** | 21 | ÷ | 7 | = | ..... | **O** | 8 | x | 6 | = | ..... |
| **C** | 45 | ÷ | 9 | = | ..... | **P** | 18 | ÷ | 9 | = | ..... |
| **D** | 10 | x | 1 | = | ..... | **Q** | 7 | x | 3 | = | ..... |
| **E** | 12 | ÷ | 3 | = | ..... | **R** | 8 | x | 7 | = | ..... |
| **F** | 4 | x | 10 | = | ..... | **S** | 8 | x | 2 | = | ..... |
| **G** | 7 | x | 9 | = | ..... | **T** | 9 | x | 8 | = | ..... |
| **H** | 8 | x | 4 | = | ..... | **U** | 6 | x | 9 | = | ..... |
| **I** | 48 | ÷ | 8 | = | ..... | **V** | 9 | x | 4 | = | ..... |
| **J** | 9 | x | 9 | = | ..... | **W** | 5 | x | 10 | = | ..... |
| **K** | 40 | ÷ | 5 | = | ..... | **X** | 9 | x | 5 | = | ..... |
| **L** | 81 | ÷ | 9 | = | ..... | **Y** | 8 | x | 10 | = | ..... |
| **M** | 49 | ÷ | 7 | = | ..... | **Z** | 10 | x | 9 | = | ..... |

The balloon will come to land in ..... ..... ..... ..... ..... ..... .....